"Ask me / for a book of doors that open all at onc
ningly, a movement back and forth — flowing, shuttling, plunging, leaping,
folding — between forms of attention and feeling, both delicate and strong, both
intricate and vast. One encounters moving focal points in flashes of particularity,
and large, elliptical orbits of unified emotional, thematic, political, and conceptual
concern. "Out there there are / fragments of voice not yet settled / to ash." Here are
lines of astonishing lucidity, and yet a deep mystery lingers within unravelings and
crystallizations miraculously deft and gorgeously slipping. And here also is great
intimacy, not only on the stage of loss, within its framework and lived experience,
but also toward precise people and places, lovingly, in affection, attachment, invo-
cation, and elegy. "And to know the sadness is to know the flame."

At times one might feel Dickinson, at times, Woolf, glass panes, shadows, the
hanging cloths of Eva Hesse—an arcing topology and groundswell of care, for
children, mothers, phantoms, friends—"... to scan the names for names I know /
no more mere than they are massive / like the weight of dust-crowned / loam." Arid
and vegetal, contained and expansive, optical and opaque, it just sings. There is an
incredible, beautiful strangeness in this fluid architecture, impossible to pin down,
always ebbing and never at rest: "Like / silence spawning music."
—Kevin Holden, author of *Pink Noise*

Like a murmuration of starlings whose contortions hover and careen before es-
cape, Julie Carr's Underscore is an ambient & pointillistic deep saturation of the
economies of twilight. In these tapering hours when we release the screwdriver
from our grip, these words emerge as beads of sweat broken from a fever. I trust
the perversity of these poems because it is a perversity so elemental that listens to
what it should not be listening to: under floorboards, the punished, the yeast. In a
necessary poetics of the ill-equipped, this book speaks to the violence and ultimate
limits of use and to somatic transmissions only possible in disintegration and power

out. As a silhouettist of language, Carr's words gather in the thousand dots from disparate frequencies, concentrating them so momentarily yet so sharply until the moving edges cut shadows into the land, out of something like the human.
—Valerie Hsiung, author of *The Naif*

The underscore—a line drawn beneath, an emphasis on top of which we move, tremble, sweat, and want. A plank we walk, both towards and away from one another, always simultaneously. Between the inbreath and the outbreath, curling in and furling out: we dance in wide absences drenched in light that is the shifting shape of our teachers. Julie Carr's stunning *Underscore* reminds us that desire is a form of participation.
—Selah Saterstrom, author of *Ideal Suggestions* and *Slab*

If the race has already begun to see which poetries might outwit AI in the coming years, perhaps a poetics of hyper-personal address might endure the longest, might be just the tech needed to code into the real. Julie Carr's *Underscore* is clusters of code-cracking poems aimed at demonstrating how the *implicit* people of our lives become the *explicit*, the actual stakes. In this, Carr's 8th book of poetry, social-psychic dissolution is momentarily snatched from the jaws of The Shredder we call American Society. And with social crises nipping at the edges of these intricate, lush poems, Carr adeptly ignores, or dodges, or straight up smacks the dizzy head of Imperium—to our delight.
—Rodrigo Toscano, author of *The Charm and the Dread.*

Also by Julie Carr

POETRY

100 Notes on Violence (Ahsahta Press, 2010; Omnidawn Publishing, 2024)
Real Life: An Installation (Omnidawn Publishing, 2018)
Think Tank (Solid Objects, 2015)
RAG (Omnidawn Publishing, 2014)
Sarah—Of Fragments and Lines (Coffee House Press, 2010)
Equivocal (Alice James Books, 2007)
Mead: An Epithalamion (University of Georgia Press, 2004)

CO-TRANSLATION

The Book of Skies, by Leslie Kaplan (Pamenar Press, 2024)
Excess—The Factory, by Leslie Kaplan (Commune Editions, 2018)

PROSE

Mud, Blood, and Ghosts: Populism, Eugenics, and Spiritualism in the American West (University of Nebraska Press, 2023)
Climate (collaborative essays with Lisa Olstein, Essay Press, 2022)
Someone Shot My Book (University of Michigan Press, 2018)
The Silence that Surrounds the Future (Essay Press, 2015)
Active Romanticism: The Radical Impulse in Nineteenth-Century and Contemporary Poetic Practice (coedited with Jeffrey Robinson, University of Alabama Press, 2015)
Surface Tension: Ruptural Time and the Poetics of Desire in Late Victorian Poetry (Dalkey Archive, 2013)

Library of Congress Cataloging-in-Publication Data

Names: Carr, Julie, 1966- author.
Title: Underscore / Julie Carr.
Other titles: Underscore (Compilation)
Description: Oakland, California : Omnidawn Publishing, 2024. | Summary:
    "Julie Carr's most intimate book to date, Underscore, is dedicated
    to two of Carr's foundational teachers, the dancer Nancy Stark Smith and
    the poet Jean Valentine, both of whom died in 2020. Elegiac and
    tender-at times erotic at other times bitter-these poems explore the
    passions of friendship and love for the living and the dead. Reaching at
    once toward the "ghost companions in the thicket" and to the beloveds
    who still "pulse with activity," Underscore's sonically intricate
    poems ultimately yearn toward a public intra-action, a sense of expanded
    encounter, what Stark Smith called "overlapping kinespherees." There, in
    the "green, green underscore," "the darkened / cloth / changes /
    hands.""-- Provided by publisher.

Identifiers: LCCN 2024002631 | ISBN 9781632431318 (trade paperback)
Subjects: BISAC: POETRY / American / General | POETRY / Women Authors
    LCGFT: Poetry.
Classification: LCC PS3603.A77425 U53 2024 | DDC 811/.6--dc23/eng/20240117
LC record available at https://lccn.loc.gov/2024002631

Published by Omnidawn Publishing, Oakland, California
www.omnidawn.com
10 9 8 7 6 5 4 3 2 1
ISBN: 978-1-63243-131-8

UNDERSCORE

Julie Carr

OMNIDAWN PUBLISHING
OAKLAND, CALIFORNIA
2024

for Nany Stark Smith and Jean Valentine, in memory

throw yourself
out of yourself

—Paul Celan

Contents

III. Dirt After Pulse

IV. I don't know who tied these knots

I. Underscore

Was the world

full of shields? Of old robes

hung heavy with daylight?

Before my birth & your electric cry

I rode in on you and on

wind, a public wind, toward the

rupture-glide

that eagle with its

white feathered round skull flies.

Cruising and wordless in its

breadth breaching river's dusk

from out of the past of the

hills, it heads down

into dust, for and of it.

7:58

Out there there are

       fragments of voice not yet settled

to ash. Disturbed hands thrust

       into hair where

there, out there there are

       sirens as lustrous swarms

fly above a bush, a thread of web spun to hang

       as spittle from an old cat's jaw

thinning

thinning, insofar as I go, I go

       somewhat sensing what that sound tells of, that cry

down the avenue, its westerly view

       veering wide with the shine on the

tar.

*

Out there

       there are sounds : my baleful

boy child girl child girl child boy

ply me with

       their fingers in food as their lashes cast shadows

like some islands do on sea.

See, I did not count the sirens but am counting them now, how they semi-weep
just south of

       the low severed sun swelling high.

The Underscore

for Nancy Stark Smith (1952–2020)

those birds white-headed black-winged unafraid
slow comical song   they call to me   I call to them

trying this key then another in the padlock
how it is always was July

scarred sidewalks   mouthless choirs ghost companions in the thicket

how the soil in the trowel folds inward like a jacket
and daughters without mothers fall backwards into bushes

raspberry fingertips tensed tongues
they test the broken edges of cups

how they work with people   how they get you ready to be touched
how the sun pours translucence into leaves

how the orange bead on a string around my neck
was an orange bead on a string around yours

how the throat beats with blood and voice
                    coursing coarse sore

in this way we serve one another
with airdropped flowers in our phones

who is missing you today? who turned your camera off?
whose plane grazed the low cloud to release the rain

that floods the back of my mirror again?

Common

5lb dumbbell   holds the poem flat
while reluctance weights the lids.

I've got   no unusual

                forms of hesitation, only the same ones

you've got too.   It wants

two bright bells to keep it from shuttering, to keep
the words from burying themselves

         like some sphinx refusing

to tell the truth about kings, the truth about peasants, the truth about fathers
and sons.
       My mouth also

takes the shape of no   a bow, an auto-run anti-Eros, cloudy ingrate,
a scrim.

         The heart thrums regard-
less pools
flush with sun   even as that sun

is now   snow falling swift between walls   hid away

and people, some people

hard kept from themselves, from the death toll   while at the meat-
                packing plant they work elbow

to elbow, breastbone to carcass

                        prepping bodies for the bodies that keep on breathing

soaked in an unlivable dream, like a desert forced luxurious like
                silence spawning music, like a common disease.

17 letters for Lisa at the start [3.12.20–4.30.20]

It was the morning all my friends texted me in despair.

-

Thinking about road trips, how we might look for a grave.

-

The first page of a book about driving to a funeral; the first page of a book about driving to a ruin. In neither case did I read further.

-

Lisa, I write into your silence, I think of you in bed. The snow drips from the branches, the house is quiet as if swathed. Salt.

-

A sentence hangs across the hall like a string of beads pulled from the throats of our mothers.

-

The sun shouts. The table hums an answer. Last night, curved into myself as if around an animal I had to protect. How are you?

-

So the street stills, the house sits, the smallest sounds echo like infant hands. They say it will snow again. Forsythia bloom alone. All the cars in their parking spots: dogs asleep in crates.

-

Lisa:

Once, I was on a beach with a journal, full of wanting for the thin, tight line of a poem, that act of deliberation—what knowledge was, the kind that only the knower knows, like the prescience of a bulb underground, a cow's tongue, the wet side of clay on a wheel. Your test came back negative but she reswabbed you. You're inside for fourteen days, that talismanic number. My kids sleep and sleep. Opening my eyes to their silence. Everything stares back, but shyly.

I found a poem from March of 2007 stuck into the pages of a cookbook. On the back side of the poem, a recipe for a custard written in my mother's hand. In 2007 she was unable to write. Therefore, the two sides of the paper do not, in time, align.

Lessen you, be summer.

A repulsive state of seeing grass.

We pretend we are ten
for a minute.

No one is like anything if we
pretend

drawings have to do with
childhood.

A palette of weapons in the
making. [3.15.2007]

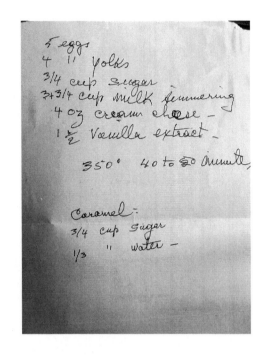

\-

Because you need to rest, I speak to you where you cannot hear me. The kids are curled or flat open: new and newish leaves. The pathogens in the house, the yeast.

\-

I revise:

Lessen you, be summer.
A repulsive state of seeing grass.
A palette of weapons in the making.

\-

Yesterday was better. Or: yesterday will have been better tomorrow.

\-

Your name like a chant in my forehead where the pain is. Your name and the pain like smoke around furniture. I took a walk, kept pulling, veering, sliding away. I told no one. It was Passover. We laughed into wine. Underneath the tablecloth, the pieces of a puzzle we will never complete. Should we mark our door with blood? Are you awake? I texted you without exclamation marks.

\-

L.

Lucy called the Prophet Elijah "that fairy girl": "Are we going to open the door for that fairy girl?" And this morning, good news about you. I quietly cheer.

Every morning I wake at precisely 2:30 and I imagine dreams I might have had, of bodies falling through water, of animals or fields or food.

-

They were singing last night. Sun comes fast. An eye, then an egg, then a face rushing toward me, which I avoid. Much the same as when I last wrote you. A song with the word God in it. I force the heat. Your text said blue, you were blue.

-

This morning Tim got out of bed and collapsed. He was unconscious for one minute, maybe less. I sat by him, my hand on his forehead, on his belly. He moved his head a little, mumbled. His eyes were not open and not shut. I said, "What is happening?" and "Can you hear me?" I got water, asked him to drink. He did and did not answer. And then, as if it had been a joke or a dream or a memory, he opened his eyes and looked at me. "What am I doing here?"

A hot day. The first hot day. I walked into the park—some maintenance workers in beige uniforms picking up the remnants of a small encampment. Blue hands. I recorded the sounds of an ambulance and of birds. A little further on, a shirtless man lay back in a low lawn chair, slowly brushing his hair.

-

A friend wrote a poem about his own death and asked me to publish it for him if needed. In the cab of the truck, a hot wind.

-

No trees have leaves, but lawns sparkle lushly. We found Alice on the floor in the hallway. Too dizzy, she said, to go to bed. But then she did. Later, music sped the room up. Orange tulips in a bit of shade. Lisa, are you warm? Is there pain? Are you sleeping?

Reckless Use (a rough-cut cento with Eigner, Bartlett, Torres, and Conrad)

I walk, I walk
the flowers seem to nod

I walk   my one good wing   warily

flutters, the flowers seem to

nod. Tag me bitter   I spill some sugar, I spill some

salt. My sister's
ill, but she's not my sister   she's my river,

her mouthpiece   tries to find an ear.
I mutter from her throat

she carries a masculine name   flanked by
birch. sycamore. brick. briar.

We walk

as the streetlamp
hoards light, as the stairwell

draws down.

Oh, I

I was just learning how to see. And what I saw, as if through fog or smoke—surrogate glances belonging to no one, wet from a sadness that had no cause. In the west where women wear white, in the east where the sun is red, in the European gardens with their lines and lawns: the uncountable absences, the holes. I found an archivist's assistant, a boy pouring mescal, mothers holding vessels, and my own mother five years underground. I was just learning to see, having passed over a massive highway like a hawk. Like other women I'd been raped and like other children I'd been hit. The air is always filling some body younger and drunker than mine, for the bellows, like a book, are never done.

As Veronica and I walked in the woods, she told me about Guillermo's grief. Two months later, Guillermo corroborated her tale. He'd been left by a woman in Boston. Homesick and alone, he was too afraid to board a plane to return. When finally he managed it, he wanted only to leave home again. Now that he had written two books, he no longer wanted to be a writer. Instead, he would reissue the old humorous novels that had gone out of print. There are, he tells us, very few funny Mexican novelists. His mission: to keep those few from falling into oblivion. Only a very sad man, says Veronica, would care so much for the jokes of the dead.

I was just learning how to see my life as if from a vantage point far off or above. There are too many books, Guillermo says, even as he labors to restore them. A woman in a zebra-striped jumpsuit fakes an animated conversation for a camera. The man who films her will soon be dead, just like me. With a popsicle stick in his back pocket and his elbows on his knees, he hangs his head.

100 days

Out-gutted and cried-out
I left the house for food.

I would, I thought, walk the alley
with a phone strapped to my forehead like a lamp.

To cough, to soak a pillow, to fake it, to yearn for the hand of a mother,
not your mother, not anyone's, an un-mother, an unknowable un-hand of an
un-mother to no one.

Our alleys are open for business—empty embraces for slower air,
empty receptacles for empty boxes

from which we pulled glass beads, pencils, soft lightbulbs, yeast, T-shirts,
medicines, filters, chocolate, rust, wrap, foam—

all of this we ingested
as our skin hardened across our soles.

I did not want to be seen.

Weather

A perfectly ordinary weather report has nothing to do with her death, or now her death enters the weather, or now she enters the weather: a piece of matter the wind makes move, or always it was this—our bodies, whether living or dead, sought after, sent with

the wind.

Wind and light, wind, light: there was the spinning moon. We always lie to get by, I said to my friends who were seated. We spoke muffled by rags, our voices meandering uneven pathways, missing ears. Our lips, being covered, could not kiss. I traced their bodies achingly—the way her foot reached under his chair, the way his thighs formed a V, a flare of skin between her belt and her

sweater. You have a hole in your skull just above your right ear. I can feel it when I caress that part of you, a dip in the skin with no bone under. A bridge without a crosser, it seems to

sway. Another friend came for flour. He straddled his bike on the sidewalk while I pried dandelions from grass. Each time I cut a root, I flung the dead thing into a can. I thought of the dog and he wagged his tail, smacking the

earth in a dream-rhythm. She died on Friday, another friend on Tuesday: weekdays with their names. I carried a stone on my head. It compressed my spine adequately. I lay on the basement floor and placed the stone on my chest; my breath labored to lift it. There was pain. The families of the dead say it's a blessing, the suffering was too much to bear. It, the suffering, was and was not born. A slit in a curtain casts a blade across the room. We will have to try harder to live, our bereaved friend said. She said this to her now fatherless sons, boys prone

to silence. When someone dies, said Ben, we redraw our map of the world. Was this what happened when Billy died, I asked? The boundaryless human unravels among grasses, moons, dogs, and sacks of plasma, moves its fingers to make sounds in the air, absorbs the scents of others who have also thrown themselves

out of themselves. I longed to touch her hair.

Coors

White gleam licks
      the west side of a pole.
          Shadow gifts

the east with a blur.
      A small pull on the inner
          wrist where the strong blue

vein falls in under flesh.
      Seated I am empty—a
          bottle with a fish mouth

gaping to the grid.
      Horses with hooves stilled
          in planetary sawdust are

what the flat fan blades resting
      were. I'm reluctant to un-
          fog the window's face

for the woman adjusting her
      strings at her neck
          I am slow.

She doesn't hold on
      any more than I do
          to the knot at her throat, she lets

it go. The other one walking
    into her glasses passes by words

meant to make us
    want beer.

River 1
for rob

roots scroll a rockface, a bit of blue above the ledge

like a bit of a roof above a man

or a bit of news keeps coming on

a bird with its beak slightly spread

and home's just a place with doors that sway

there's not much left in the snowmelt late-

leaf-laced ice—there's a branch

     *

of the Platte that swings northward

as if somehow the earth reversed its spin

         while you were driving, you thought, toward Denver

and the headaches that plague you

     flow backward through your skull   to snag the silver maple like barbed wire at the pant leg of a boy.

You thought you might cry out the pain if you cried long enough but instead it
　　　　seemed to gather

more tightly around the right temple with each pulse

　　　　　　　　　　down at the river

　　　*

with a word said twice

flat as a paper plate on a shelf

as the water makes a tunnel for its own release　　like my hand on her thigh

saying no, you're not parts to be assessed you are complete as you immerse

yourself in the clamor of sky's north-leaning

assumption. And then the phone alarms: a photo of a little girl in orange

who is lost who is ours—

she is legion, feathery and various and

　　　*

lost. I woke to the snow, how it paints

                the top sides of sturdy limbs and draws

the soft boughs down

toward the something that is new.

Heat

Amassing meta   data spins

the world's soul. When it's not me it's

telling me whose heat rises, how

the heat hangs out in a cloud, how

the heat mounts a kid's future and

rides it

to some sedimented end. The way

I wait for sleep, the way I wake

and rise, venture outside, the way

I twist my wrist, the way

"it all / no matter what / gets

away."

Our gate hangs low   and will not latch

it lets us go

to where a beam meets those sun-gathered teens.

They shine,   their legs unfold.

How I bury my gusts in my

almost adamantine will

to scan the names for names I know

no more mere than they are massive

like the weight of dust-crowned

loam.

Out of the lost   age of applause

comes a flash of my brother's laugh.

It's slow to suture then it slips.

Men meet then sit   the hot thing thinks

left of this clod   I with my hoe

collapse.

II. Use me up

Good morning

for Peter

Good morning smudged glass on the medicine chest
Good morning sea of eyes, sea of shadows
It's to you and to every bit of summer's must
that I've got my mind with my breathing
It was to find you today that I started this
this breath in a line of sound
was always to find the sound of you
or the shuffle of your stance like an apology
Good morning to the dog with his nose in the air
to the park on my right side with its memory
the shade of you and the shade of me
slipping on ice with our hands linked
How a party for you was a party for me
how I thought of your voice in some daisies
your voice that hangs out on the basement stair
sometimes I go sit beside it
That's when the world gets all swirly
when I've got you with a smoke on a fire escape
got you at a picnic of crackers and oranges
since you are to me what this is
What might seem minimal is really maximal
I position myself toward you for all of it

Sentences I've often said

The unmanifested face was my mother's and I kissed it.
She was very near phobic so we kept things quiet.

With a pencil in my mouth I wrote on my tongue: loved, unloved.

I am hypocritically awake.

Seam/Seem

In the fall of 1970 when I was three, we lived in a house at the end of a dead end we would soon leave. It was a dark house, dark on the outside and dark on the inside—its walls of deep brown shingle, its windows shaded by enormous trees. An old woman lived upstairs, and it seemed I never saw her but once. While rain blurred the windows she appeared in the hallway carrying cookies under foil, her hair white and floating, a pink dress with a belted waist. She was after that a kind of ghost, an obscurity that filled the hall at all times. Men came, they came at night and left in the morning and I remember none of them, only all of them, as if one man in different bodies but faceless. They were faceless but large because I was small, and large because my mother was small, a small woman, vulnerable in ways I knew nothing about. It was fall, I went to school, a place of hiding. Under the piano, under the nap blanket, inside the bathroom stalls I hid to suck without censor and I hid to sleep, for in my bed in the dark house, I did not sleep easily. All along the zipper seam of my yellow sleeping sack, loosened threads entwined themselves between my fingers and toes. At the window, vines tentacled toward me. I lay stiffly.

Across the end of that dead end lived a pair of scientists who had two sons. Their house was even darker than ours, its windows black, its hallways completely shrouded. From the depths of the house came shouting, maybe even screaming. I did not approach but stared from our stoop while my brother ran in and out of that door with the two sons trailing as if nothing at all was wrong.

We call our parents, our parents call

to the strings in our limbs

to the roses of our fingertips

five for my fathers, five for my mothers

under this pan-

creatic sky   they stopped

the traffic—ICE, accident, or drug bust—

we never saw we went on home

our lips are weak muscles

come in before the doors all close

Apples
for Patti Seidman (1944–2022)

I was making apple bread for Patti when my neck went out.

When there seems nothing to be done but to feed someone.

"A lot of denial around here," she wrote and I ignored it.

Wrapped the bread in foil and put it in a box.

Dancers feel their animal nature by lying on the floor.

The earth pulls the blood down and the heart resists.

This time I swore I would not allow.

There'd been five whose faces no longer.

Held sway is an expression that comes to mind.

The apples so abundantly bunched, they for the twigs: a threat.

Was it unnatural? Obscene? A kind of overkill?

Faces I knew like the back of my busy, hot, private, vulnerable, foreign, and faraway hand.

I would not allow her to leave me is a confused object.

Like a dinner plate in a bookshelf, or a glass of coiled guitar strings.

I keep saying five, but there were six.

For how do we count the faces of the dead?

How he bound toward me across the café floor.

How her lap held a sugar scent and her eyes lined blue.

The sixth was a child, skinnier than his brother and speedier.

I would not let her leave me is a confused objection.

For what I've got in this kitchen, this garden, this city ecology, this situation

is no say.

For friendship

Tell the rocks   (for lack of women)
of our river rushing its shadows

across our eyes—
how we buried what we wanted in our bodies.

> *(Don't leave your childhood, and its / sorrows)*

The soil smelled like shit
as I walked a word into the current, glistening, urban and shaking

beneath the hospital's windows and saw
myself there.

A poem on probability for Ruth

Our world goes nowhere except its own elsewhere

What kind of sentence is that?

No one is responding, but everyone is vibrating with address

all of us stationed before the same absence

like glass sheets, we see right through us to the air

The bald child

is a failed clairvoyant

but only she can penetrate this great vascular

system. Mathias kisses Lucy's head while I allow

a slow relation

between addiction and adore

River 2

where girls test ice, tapping boot heels against shine
where masked, they swing
where long fronds bend toward the duck pond's lip
I'd been reading about boys online in their secret spaces they
give each other hard-ons talking about raping fat Jews
I'd been thinking about my mother's face when she
by something she'd read or remembered was made afraid
when we walked into a crowd of history's predatory glances,
we knew them, they were
as if our friends
They stand, hold the ropes and rock
until the swings jump the air, their torsos nearly horizontal
like wings

For Patrick on his fifteenth birthday

You sing—a courage.

Politics follows what is painfully

beautiful but it's only a distraction

from your blossom-ness, your

unfurling. I write across the hole we always wake inside of

to the trees, to the fountains,

to the botanists with moths in their skirts,

to the girls still dizzy from nineteenth-century violence

crammed with no enemy they can name

and to you as you

with your sotto voice replenish

the stores that have been from you and from them

for so long withheld.

Trustworthy

If I alphabetized all these utterances, then we'd see what really makes me cry:
the entering and exiting of admirable souls.

My mother turned her face to the window, to the red-tailed hawk.

In a dream of a party in my own house that I had not planned, was not prepared
for, the guests were all in black as if at a funeral, standing and looking
       around.

I foraged for food, for something, even crackers with nothing on them, to put out
on the table.

Waking: the phrase *every man for himself.*
The word: *trustworthy*

& in the eyes

a birth, a slap, a bone-ache in the head-zone & pink lights
up the absent one. She came to me benevolently

walking through water, smiling in purple wet
T-shirt and underwear. That was one type

of mother, another fell me from a tree with a smack.

& in the eyes of road-bound wanderers it's January, it's
17 and sunny, sweet potatoes rotted out from inside

a black coat on cardboard and piles of boy-clothes
a guy with a tray of red rice on a bike.

Oh Jesus, Michael with his cancer-voice begs

forgiveness for asking (over tuna and coke) why
can't they just move if the neighborhood gets too

pricey? But it's not on me to forgive someone, I'm a Jew
we don't do it that way. We're like: if your mother were wet

would you rub her dry with your wet arms or would you
in your half sleep shake her

wanting from your head?

1.17.15

Carolyn Grace (1939–2015)

That winter was as it was supposed to be—very cold.

They could not unearth a sliver of earth from the earth
for six days & we

could not penetrate one another's eyes until the mercury rose.

But our hands were ready like children or ancient ones called for lunch.
She *returned,* I believe, on a Saturday or maybe a Friday. I'd been in a kiss

for Lucy when I heard. Lucy would try to mend
the rift in the circle now torn. Lucy, we said, only could.

Intermediate body

for Lucy

Out of her mouth comes a mirror
a fly with its summering wing

skirting the driveway's cracked tar-patch
her breath is a beat into mine

She hip-turns heel-thumps for "beauty"
she drinks from a glass I will pour

Poor acrobat spins on a future
of sweat-scented sleepover girls

I did not invent her
        I moved myself toward her, her cloud-dense outer, other, route

Like moss spreads this daughter fills broken
gaps of a ruin's wall

she's a value, a voice, a visitor

her chest thrumming green, almost see-through
where I put my ear, I put my ear

and have no plans to grieve

Like being born

& the things of a house are made of sand,

of soil of lime and of wood,

of soil of steel of wax.

An old maple shoots from the roots at the property line

like animus & a pretty girl is iron now, so blasted

she's oil from olive and olive from twigs,

twined as if combatants. Wax is what

the moon will do when I kiss you and hold

the heat in your head & I is just a word

I put on my tongue as Ma and Rosie

run the food bank with rapid speech and cardboard boxes

onions, sprouting potatoes, baby

food for local babies, bread

from warehouse ovens on a highway.

I fold the cloth, I lay the cloth, I hang the clothes

for women.

Doorless, just now

The wind tears hard at it, writes Gillian, my friend

in fires and in love. It's so dark I can't see

her yard or road or her

so dark the moon is not the sun is not   there

are no stars no lamp was set, all wicks wide away

writes Emily my guide when I was small. I would

go to the river to sleep would go to the river

with animals and pens, the wind

roughed the Charles but not the gaseous deep into which

one should never swim. On a bed over threat

under threat I curled on my side—

a dry root, an origami

box of gusts. I was I am an American

at war forever: for space, for heat, for money.

Seasonal Poem

Rooks in autumn: a pair of roughed and lowered gisarmes
    repair my stack of hours
                Cricket in the curtain
erotically abloom asters:

is nakedness a virtue?   Ware and worn
slumped over the piano, the unavoidable verdict murmuring on

as reasons for getting rid of bodies
ally themselves

to protesters in Bangor until
                all forces unify

at the end.

River 10

for Jon Easley (1966–1998)

I got street-drunk like Baudelaire. Fell asleep on a lawn with my friend Jon.

The muddy river's kick back
the bridge lights and the neon moon.

Around here drought draws the mule deer down
to the fences against which watered rose vines grow.

Insomniac wind fucks the hours, the youngest
graze our crumbs—the so meager and so dry.

Hunger's what the dog knows, what the mule deer and the jay
but I know the lost scent of one who did not stay.

Morning weekday sky cornea
  for L, A, B, and T

From skate-rink pink to ballroom blue to

postrevolution ashen heft : I survive to see

such things, to press my heel to wood.

Today's list of broken things—lamp, switch, door,

knee, nipple, neighborhood. Today's store of what

refuses to dissolve : love, lying shit

of a president, child-spring, and clouds now

fictional in the back-mind of memory

where forgotten words—

talus and crypt and a word for what binds

so tirelessly the five of us,

our sounds sliding up through the stairway's gloom—reside.

Our gray eyes or our green, or that

sweet brown and that

blue : they bloom and also shine and see across the room,

wet with the body's terminable water.

River 3

and to know the sadness is to know the flame

that forms in the hand as if the rodent

beneath the rock broke back into its body

to roam

to know

the body insofar as the body's ungovernable

is to know how it turns in on itself after it's done leaving itself

behind

I insofar as I was, was steadied at the foot of a bridge

by his arm, was directed toward what would be

an earthly home, where we, a five-person person, would gather

but first there would have to be

a bicycle

in the dark, spokes upshone like the river itself

tossing office fluorescents skyward in waves, this was

long before the terror war, long before

my body insofar as it was one was torn by

infant heads on

being born

for first there had to be

a flood in the throat, a tidal mouth spreading to the bay

and I in as much as I was was pliant, would make myself

like a pet or a man or an ancient oar

in an oarlock moan

In a thicket

The world's tucked tight in a thicket

-

the old ridden-over world

-

So suck the thicket

-

spit out the world

-

One warbler, a blue, a blur

-

Her slow song uses me

-

up like a brand

III. Dirt After Pulse

It

She said it's not done with you yet. I agreed, but had no way to approach it, to find out what it wanted from me that it had not yet got. The day was decidedly unmagical, mundanity in the gray of sky, in our waiting-stance that nonetheless pulsed with activity. Not that we were so busy at that time of year, but that we were anticipating business and also a death. Hauled the tree to one side. Scattered salt. Cleaned the water of the water. Felt a little Jesus. Felt a little egg. We watched a rape movie, curling further into our selves. Soon, we would disperse.

Once I tried to notate the thumb-suck of childhood, the rubbing and the climbing, the watching. My brother's breath furred the other side of a wall. My sister's sardonic hair-toss and the way she ran when they tried to force her into a skirt. Our parents had had us. Had had it and us. Through the rain, I watched a truck slide by. It was packed with loaves. The face on its side was of a girl like me. Fat cheeks as if stuffed. Could I, might I, eat her?

In the bath, as the water cooled, I texted my friend: where are you? She texted back from the back of her daughter. She too was lonely and wildly protective of love, both hers and mine. They, she and her husband with the raspy voice, had been driving in the 1990s too fast. Pulled over for gas where she found herself squatting to piss among bent grasses and dog shit. Sunglasses propped on her head, heart beating blood into outer parts.

But what was it that was, as she'd said, still wanting? I'd been on a winter beach looking for shells with a man whose birthday we'd celebrated the night before when she said that. In a Chinese restaurant, he and eight women had sat in a circle. Each of you, he'd said, passing the rice, has sucked my dick. The women laughed wondering if it was true. It was not. I'd been in his room but had not gone down. Not literally and not figuratively. I felt now empty, still not low, not nearly low enough. Hovering as if falling asleep to a roll call, I was waiting for it to be finally near to me, with me, and with me done.

After the Convention, 2016
for Gillian

After the convention we drove east and I slept.

                      After the convention, the many cops in their dances
their dances on horses, on foot, on bikes, their dances in blue,
in camo, in beige

we needed to laugh on the highway but we did not after the convention
laugh.

Buffalo rose up into a rainlessness all day
time takes all of the time

you wrote and I read from my lap.
                      We'd walked under no rain and there was

no rain now neither—it was hot then hot now there was

after the convention a full moon
to the right of us, felt it bob and move and maybe comment if it could

as a drive-by hauled a mower to a lawn where

white guys stood smoking, talking low and looking down
as a black guy walked, eyes straight

                                ahead, and all day through the day
that heat kept rising and won't even now let up.

Panel II

after Nancy Spero

Begin again, or whatever this morning drink means to you, morning sink, this
cloud they're still selling

       as if profit could alter the mirror

as if profit could drift over floorboards   as women marry their dresses
                or shelter in meadows to bleed

when our brothers enter
our mouths with their skin-shields

we are only fit to detach

     *

On her body he took his stand comes at me, rough like   summer's effort
to spoil

as my future detox shifts toward

elegy and my heart tightens for
greater security

in its acid home

*

We were girls; we sat in her living room and were served
She was old

she played us a video of workers painting the underbelly of a dome
her assistant gave us

cookies   we were girls in a time of war, which was

only the aftertaste of other wars
to come

*

to bleach her shoes, her teeth, her hair, her face, he took his stand

*

If sleep could deliver a saddle,

a stem, or an ordinary   child's body-roll

but dumb morning deals   only women's faces in profile, mouths open
like gutters

we were girls, we lifted our arms to the night sky, the city's
street slid southward

through our bicycle wheels   we photographed ourselves as   dulled arrows

we slept uneasy
under the lean scent of men's thighs

Spectacular leap

The hard thing lifts with you in it.
What is the air but a delivery service for less

Medicaid, SNAP, & housing for kids.
The thing you're in humps the chill above snowed-up mounds of earth and stone
Her makeup kit jumps her lap

Cords twine in their readiness to move
word of cold

cuts to your ear: less
mediocre care for whoever hasn't got

a home or a job or a bone.

Liberation file

By sheer accident we fell in love with it (the world).
Humiliation flares between you and me (whoever is on top).

Outside one

learns to see through things
like the rich
soil pumped so nearly dry I crave
lung lift Ella's broken love
poem to pulse up
from that underswell now
drawn so far down like the life span
of a dog, it throbs.

Post-debate

The hours between 3 and five are mine or are to me to me alone—a shaking
        of dirt from a rag. Was it dragged, it was, across mantel until matted

until it mattered less if I slept, mattered less and less, my lips
        gathered against breathing.

I'd likewise forgotten what my body knew which was how it was to make
        one—a body, a girl, a hurst, hump, torqued tongued

baby. The hours between then and now are not mine no longer and
        the longer no rest arrives the more of me I lose. So go

cast against couch cushion, I'm not
        rising or pushing, not boning up for the dereliction called day. This

apophatic face faces a crack
        that lets no light in.

Artificial Hells

Snow is patchy and dirty snow, patchier. One
tree leans; two split in two. Ask me
whether the keys rattling in someone's hand
are a utopian orientation toward glossier hopes,
if footprints make ghosts out of crystals,
if the drumbeat comes up from below or
down from above. Ask me

for a book of doors that open all at once,
a book of radios arguing with pianos,
for fountains side by side like hollow homes for
memories of candy-mouthed kids.

Snow tightens into eyeballs, into ears and
onto lips, now ask me
something about this artificial Hell gleaming
off a man's crown as he bends
toward the echo of a no-no horn
in a winter skirt swaying as the woman slides
her wheeled walker down.

Dear Senator

Falling waves and full-throated fumes
do not care about you.

Blonde horses, blind
waves rise and do not

care about you.

Our sister does not
in her flushed face want

what you want
at all.

        *

There's a light in a room three rooms away.
I'm not I'm never going to turn it off.

This sapling night's steeped in that

puddle   where the green green
underscore

plays for free.

Father's Day

through the glass

my elbow

smells of lake and old navy boy

and dad in matching

T's   I'd found a knife

from a different era

convenient   store

water in my

car.   I had a child   needed that water,

they always do.   All doors

we'd thought we'd   locked

slid open   the private bed was

broken   in two.

how might I keep my kids at home, how might I keep them safe asked the women who

held each other   off.   It was

freedom-day a day

like all days   a

thunderous roll, holding hands   everything talking   running rain

through our hair.   The boy and his dad

had slogans on their chests: *the cops*

love us. It was

father's day   father's night.   At least,

someone said, they know how it works.

Future conditional

would that there might be a cool red thread   drawn through all the faces
in this crowd

would that the barricades might be
removed re-

made as trellises   for rivers
        to go on   to go on   the crowd has fallen, face down

Would that they might rise from the heaviness of bones
                to the future-light of windows   open, gasping washes of air

If you're feeling good, says one woman from the back, her voice hot, hotter,
run to it. run to it.   it's an "afterlife"

        *

danced before us
a small hole in her stomach and her heels
like orbs of moonlight on water.

        *

my daughter sleeps with her beloved all morning; all night she moves through
        these streets

for a little while   she slept on my chest   rises and falls with my lungs.

Then it was Wednesday's "hour of lead," I could no longer
move my blood. I put everything down, including my arms

while pole beans sent out their curling stems

      *

Friday came, shoveling dirt.

Ma's husband works at the chicken factory
where only the young have kept their jobs.

She places milk bottles in the forty boxes
I do the lettuce, ziplocked from the garden, while Don

with one hand steadies his back, with the other,
apples. Ma's baby girl

had been ripped from her arms and right there, before her, shot dead.

      *

That night the creek rose full   that night we followed
the tuba and the snare

That night, the cool red thread   would run
through our open mouths if our mouths were   through our ears

if our ears were if open.

Between our poor day and the great night

I looked for a line in CDMX but there was just the sound of sweeping

across a brightly lit room and a man looked up. This was as ever what it was.

Outside, evening was coming—traffic and my feet were colder.

An old man played his body with a bow.

The highest notes came from the top of his head where the hair had thinned.

I have not been gentle. Where I was hurt, I hurt my daughter.

No one should feel sorry for me. César Vallejo, I don't deserve your company.

Dirt after Pulse
for K.J.

It gets so dark you know, K.J.,
beneath us where the words aren't

but I danced anyway, a kind of swing, just think
of bugs bunny, of the sky, voluptuous and silly—

it's what they were when they died
is what I am with you beside—

a girl all dressed in green
her hair below her shimmering

ass, she too was told to lie low. It gets
so dark K.J. you know, and why must

the dancing kids, the praying kids, the hanging out kids
at this time and at these hands

where the red dirt is, where the words are not
where we will one day be.

One point seven million

afternoon begs escape

as rain chills the sheets

gears are stripped and girls

hollowed hollered

loud across the park's swollen

meadow where our trammeled

green veers to fever

like the open mouths of crowns

set to shimmer

on murderous heads

Friday day Friday night

Day's Garamond 10 in the eugenic stride
of pissed-off job lines and anti-home-ec
handouts. Sky's so hard blue it's unbalanced forcing the earth like a
bitch in the park's pathways chained to her human's
hand. Platinum platted cruddier dolls fall forward toward the torn edge
of a box. We've got underwear in a stroller and tomato stalks stalled in the dirt.
Come. Come on. Rick's giving letterpressed vote signs away
& Blair's RAD AIDers are out with their alt-cop flier for free.
Night's ashy & hopeful & deep. We go there, our faces
flash, rushed with new blood.

Chatter parade

Scandals

hide

the

craven

crumbs

wanting

slivers

time

the darkened

cloth

changes

hands.

IV. I don't know who tied these knots

Night

To walk: the dark barely
breathable, the air hangs

is hanging   an animal

rots within the stone
walls of this foundation

as if a chapter torn from a slowly uploading document.

I am told the system encountered a problem, that where people are most afraid
there is no boat, no boat, no campground, no grocery store.

I will find the rotting thing. I was looking at a broad leaf as I said this
and then it started to rain

is raining like never before,
the stench and its origins untraceable. Fathers are moles, are otters, are egrets

and garlands
of honeysuckle, dandelion and petty

malice   are fathers. Our father
sleeps through this air though this air is mostly

water.   Some people do live long enough
to make themselves in others   an accident of un becoming

just as

the moss takes my footprint only to release it

back outward to   some blue
heron and some rose

                              hips bowing, bowed
like defeated archers by the sea.

Don't

The dog's limping again. Don't talk to me

when I'm like this, singing
in falsetto harmony like a boy-band

with my ex-friend's sister's hair-strand
in my throat. Look

at that lawman, how he stands
so stock-still with his glasses on—

first thing I saw in the wine store
was his gun.

Dirty water: Montrose, Colorado

Once without sleep or   enough of it   I spread my unreliable thigh

for one green-tailed towhee to hop on   briefly she   with her three
toes staked

an indelible claim   of invitation on the human

skin   So many shuttered shops

for clothes and toys, frames and flowers, books, tools, measuring cups, nothing

you can't get at Target in 2020   This singular hot silent sun-raged
farm-town street won't soon again

or ever

In the winter of 1906   a man built a fruit storage and packing
house in the side of this gulch

15 rods north of his dwelling

Walls were of red brick and doubled with air space   ceiling of sheet metal,
eight inches of sawdust on top

I could keep apples or potatoes all winter very nicely   while inside the
canyon's black shadows the Gunnison

cold, diverted, ran thinner—

I swam that day without moving my limbs   to serve

my bare foot to the floor   of this soft delirious valley made green
by a war made by men

who knew nothing at all of all that would   come to fail to be.

A letter

The noise in the street was a very big noise.
They shot tear gas into the train car.
300 people lost their eyes.

Dear Stephen,

Might you recommend an author or two who has something to say
about desire, fear, anger, love, and the sweetness of a four-year-old
girl's voice in the night?

Dear Stephen,

The world is a series of refrains, keeping time with heartbeats and
no. Forget that.

Meager clump of weeds

tossed after gathered as sunlight

blanched the SUVs dragging beneath them

their shade and Yasmeen on a stone

fronted the flickering sea. We'd sped past

the sardine factory and our grandmother's birthplace

like gulls holding steady against gusts. What glittered

was her infant wrist and not

what it had born.

I don't know who tied these knots

We've been complaining about the same thing for as long as
we've been complaining which is long. The boy lowers himself to the floor
and on his knees, jumps. I wanted to write a poem to the future
unborn whose air I've been using, to write a poem to my dead mother
whose air I've also been using. At her stone
on her birthday, we talked about landlords. The hills held
new corpses, winged ants swarmed a name. It was fall, I needed
sunglasses, my son was excited about the sky. After you, says a young man
with low boots to an old one in a coat. It was good to be born
at least at first, says a woman with a four-footed stick. She makes her masked way
her silver earrings sway. I hiked a hard trail and sat on a ridge.
No amount of sweat or view seemed to ask me to live, but with them
I washed my face.

New Year

for Jean Valentine (1934–2020)

The basement, green and cold behind three doors: here was
the middle one
which you know.

In whitewashed walls, your hand had curved around its pen.
It was your kitchen where you draw your brows
and the phone rang: your daughter.

She wanted you to go to an appointment to check your head.
You laughed. I remember things, you said, I'm sitting here with.

Said my name, but it was a question. It was the night
we became again human: though tired, though old, though you did not call back

through the whole night, though I had to be
in a different room, "chewing up the mirror."

In the morning, you had a gift for us: a compass on a long chain
which you wore when you skipped ahead of me, descending into the station.

River 4

for Tim

After tongue in you, the window folds.

This is the heat for which the debt ceiling rises

as the breath of decades flows inward like an apology long held back.

*

After fat felt markers drew their vapor trails on newsprint, we let them,

uncapped, fall to the earth where the roots, relentless

in their water search, seething, maybe, are.

No one can drink ocean-water, no one can drink lichen—

I put my plastic sheen on to block the drying-out function

as arbitrarily my neck, belly, vagina, sole, elbow-crease, and lower-lip

were done.

*

Court rules no to the welfare

law, no to the

free womb and no holding back

from punishing the punished.

Lick honey from my finger while remembering a dream

in which a child's face is half-covered with fungi, and I

with a long needle inject the cure

straight into her cheek.

*

After all, the years enfold,

as cupping the back of your skull with one hand, the other

the injured one, tucked

all at once we're on that bridge's on-ramp,

as the waters make some flashing scene

where for us, prenatally,

everything begins that will end.

Omaha, 2019

Nothing was purchased but my nipple was
hard, nothing was sold, but solid was the
sun on our heads. There were three dancing and
one was a vet and one had ink
running down her face and one had seen me
sliding under the bath.
The dance would decide whose face caught the light
and while the flag tried to warp us, we'd not been born
on purpose and she, Bea, was beautiful with her
mom, a new mom, a temp mom, a beloved
dancefloor mom. I got lost on my way
got caught in the grassy sway a man's
wrist floating from his seat on the lawn.
Unfurl, furl, billow, blow: no one cared
what that cloth had to say.

Just now: burning

I've driven clean through this rough beloved
morning: what carries me to you.

Give me your glance, your finger stroke, your fine first name
to burn in the post-light light.

What's in my eye is on repeat my organs on reverse
my sex is on my mind on tour, my bones so barely held.

My body's winter blaze made steadily erect by you.

Dear Listener

I didn't know what I was doing or why I was doing it.
Perhaps you guided me as if a path through deep grass, as if the color blue

episodic flare—

and there were bags, baggage unclaimed
and other women watching me, they seemed hurt—I had, I knew it,

hurt them in some way. I was ill, I would have slept
longer still, but that I was on the highway,

the highway had a place for me to fill,
so that when I came then to find you, I was late.

Listener, no striving, in a sense, no choosing. I arrived,
tiny weeds in my fingers, dirt in the skin of my hands.

A monarch appeared behind me—a girl in the spray of the hose.

These things are real, I'm telling them to you
though I've wanted to diminish them, to turn myself

harder. I am light,
she said, I am stretchy, I feel like nothing and it feels so good.

I feel like nothing, like I am nothing. I could play for 49 hours,

for 49 hours and 59 minutes, and I would even play
for 50 hours if you asked me to, if I had to, she said.

Listener, you are forbidden, far, and unreal until
I make you up by telling you

what she said.

A Note on Title and Dedication

Nancy Stark Smith's "The Underscore" is an improvisational dance practice, performed by people all over the world. It begins, as all dances do, in stillness. But not stillness. It begins with the body moving with the air and the earth, with the pulse and the warmth of blood running through veins. It begins in falling into gravity and spinning with planetary motion. After falling comes rising, the rebound. One might begin to activate within the skin, to aerate by shaking the fluids in the body, by requesting a quicker exchange between the chambers of the heart and the lungs. Small motion leads to larger motion: the limbs extend, find their edges, and move beyond those edges toward the surrounding space. With this expansion, the surround also expands. Eventually one begins to engage, not only with the floor and the space nearby, but also with the space surrounding other bodies in the room. Nancy called this "overlapping kinespheres." There is grazing, brushing, attraction, repulsion, encounter, and engagement. With engagement, there is extended touch, weight, pressure, risk, both trust and fear, and release. Here is both finding and losing, the core dynamic of encounter.

Nancy was my teacher for about ten years, starting in 1987 when I met her at a dance workshop outside of Santa Fe, New Mexico. In the mid 1990s, Nancy and I, along with Chris Aiken, Peter Bingham, Jeff Bliss, and Ray Chung, formed an improvisational performance group we called "Group Six." Everyone had other stuff going on, but we managed to practice and perform together in multiple cities over a period of about four years. The tension between individual style, desire, expertise, even aggression, and group listening, support, collaboration, and confluence—that tension, which is alive in all social spaces—classrooms, workplaces, families, cities—was, in my memory now, the dances' subject, their reason.

Nancy had many gifts. One of them was to awaken a sense of gravitas, of deep meaning, in all who met and danced with her. She was one of the world's great listeners; she listened with her whole being. But she was also one of the most dynamic talkers I will ever know. She was, in short, a purveyor of the power of exchange.

During that same decade, the 1990s, I was gathering also with a different group of people. We met regularly to share our writing, to try to teach each other what it might mean to make a poem. Sometimes we invited poets we admired to attend our meetings as a kind of temporary teacher. One of these poets was Jean Valentine. During those sessions, and for twenty years of subsequent friendship—weekends spent in her New York apartment, reading each other's drafts, discussing other poets we were reading, walking out to find food on upper Broadway, then returning to read and talk some more—Jean taught me one thing, but it's the most important thing. For Jean, what mattered in a poem was its emotional or spiritual center. The rest, she was less interested in. While she might admire flamboyant displays of language, might enjoy formal experimentation or narrative line, none of this was essential to her. Poetry was a way into the interior, and that interior, which one could call God if one wished to (and she sometimes did), was unknowable and ineffable by definition. The most important aspect of writing was its ability to indicate what it cannot ever say. "Poem without words / world electric with you."

These were my teachers; they still are. Every poem in this book is dedicated to them, for every poem has tried, in one way or another, to respond to the teachings they offered. I say "tried" but it is much less directed than that. The real teachers enter you. What you need from them resides within you as an unforgettable, permanent truth. Nancy's and Jean's teachings live, almost like hormones, within my body. Both women died in 2020. I hope their spirits are somehow spoken here.

Acknowledgments

Thanks are due to the editors of *High Country News, Interim, Oversound, Poem-a-Day, Poetry, Tupelo Quarterly*, and *Volt* for publishing several of these poems, often in earlier versions, in their journals and websites.

Thank you to readers Gillian Conoley and Lisa Olstein for your deep understanding, inspiration, and guidance. Huge thanks to rob mclennan for the collaboration that sustained me through the worst part of lockdown and that led to the "River" poems. Thank you to Rusty and Laura for all your continued dedication, support, passion, and care. Thank you Ken, in memory, for all that you gave so many of us. Thank you to Tim Roberts for the cover design, and thank you to Shanna Compton for the interior design. Thank you to all the friends mentioned in these poems and all the ones not mentioned but who are here, nonetheless. You know who you are and I love you. As always, thank you to Lucy, Alice, Benjamin, and Tim for everything and all of it.

Notes

"Throw yourself / out of yourself": Paul Celan, *Last Poems*, 39. Trans. Katharine Washburn and Margret Guillemin. San Francisco: North Point Press, 1970.

"It all / no matter what / gets away": Nathaniel Mackey, *School of Udhra*, 62. San Francisco: City Lights Books, 1993.

"Don't leave your childhood, and its / sorrows": Etel Adnan, *Time*, 23. Trans. Sarah Riggs. New York: Nightboat Books, 2019.

"Between our poor day and the great night": Cesar Vallejo, *The Complete Poetry*, 227. Trans. Clayton Eshleman. Berkeley: University of California Press, 2007.

"Chewing up the mirror": Jean Valentine, "The Locked Ward: OT," *The Cradle of the Real Life*, 60. Middletown, CT: Wesleyan University Press, 2000.

"Poem without words / world electric with you": Jean Valentine, "Poetry," *The Cradle of the Real Life*, 53. Middletown, CT: Wesleyan University Press, 2000.

About the Author

Julie Carr is the author of twelve previous books of poetry and prose. She has collaborated with dance artists K.J. Holmes and Gesel Mason, and with poet and filmmaker Carolina Ebeid. With Tim Roberts she is the co-founder of Counterpath Press, Counterpath Gallery, and Counterpath Community Garden in Denver.

Underscore

by Julie Carr

Cover design by Tim Roberts
Interior design by Shanna Compton

Cover typeface: Didot
Interior typeface: Adobe Garamond Pro

Printed in the United States
by Books International, Dulles, Virginia

Publication of this book was made possible in part by gifts from
Katherine & John Gravendyk in honor of Hillary Gravendyk,
Francesca Bell, Mary Mackey, and The New Place Fund

Omnidawn Publishing   Oakland, California

Staff and Volunteers, Fall 2023

Rusty Morrison senior editor & co-publisher
Laura Joakimson, executive director and co-publisher
Rob Hendricks, poetry & fiction editor, & post-pub marketing
Jason Bayani, poetry editor
Anthony Cody, poetry editor
Liza Flum, poetry editor
Kimberly Reyes, poetry editor
Sharon Zetter, poetry editor & book designer
Jeffrey Kingman, copy editor
Jennifer Metsker, marketing assistant
Sophia Carr, marketing assistant
Katie Tomzynski, marketing assistant